Easy Christian Crafts Preschool/Kindergarten

by
Linda Standke

Cover illustration by
Jack Snider

Illustrations by
Julie Anderson

Carson-Dellosa Christian Publishing

Scripture taken from the HOLY BIBLE: NEW INTERNATIONAL VERSION®. NIV®. Copyright © 1973, 1978, 1984 by International Bible Society. Used by permission of Zondervan Publishing House.

The "NIV" and "New International Version" trademarks are registered in the United States Patent and Trademark Office by International Bible Society.

Credits:
Author: Linda Standke
Project Director: Sherrill B. Flora
Editors: Sherrill B. Flora, D'Arlyn Marks, Sharon Thompson
Cover Illustration: Jack Snider
Cover Design: Annette Hollister-Papp
Inside Illustrations: Julie Anderson

ISBN 0-88724-794-6

Introduction

This book was designed for parents, home educators, Sunday school, and Christian school educators who want to provide fun and rewarding craft projects that teach young children about God's love.

Your little ones will learn so much as they walk the animals into the ark, place baby Jesus in the stable, and roll the stone away from Jesus' tomb. The projects included in this book not only allow children to learn Bible truths from easy-to-make craft projects, but they also provide children with play experiences that promote the telling and retelling of favorite Bible stories.

Each craft project begins with a scripture reference and a short summary to help guide the parent/teacher. Read the entire Biblical passage, discuss its meaning with the children, and then follow up with the craft activity.

It is the author's hope that as you guide the children through these craft projects, they will learn about and experience God's love.

Contents

Days of Creation Lace-Up Cards

Genesis 1

Let your young children have the fun of celebrating creation as they make these wonderful lace-up cards.

Materials Needed:

* ✳ Heavy card stock
* ✳ Paper punch
* ✳ Yarn
* ✳ Crayons or markers
* ✳ Masking tape
* ✳ Scissors

Directions:

1. Copy the lace-up card patterns found on pages 5 through 8 onto card stock.
2. Color the patterns and cut out the cards.
3. Punch holes on the small circles on the pattern.
4. Using a small piece of masking tape, wrap the end of a piece of yarn several times to make a sturdy end for lacing.
5. Tie a knot in one end of the yarn. Have the children begin lacing through the back of the pattern so the knot is on the back of the card. Wrap the yarn around the edge bringing it down and through the next hole on the card. Continue until the card is completely laced.
6. Leave one end of the yarn unknotted to allow the children to pull out the yarn and replace their cards as many times as they desire.

3.   Punch Holes

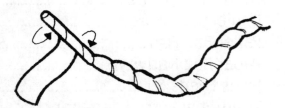

4. With masking tape, wrap the end of a piece of yarn to create a safe needle.

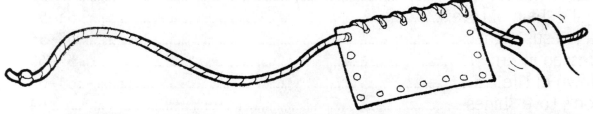

5.   Tie a knot in one end of the yarn. Have the children begin lacing through the back of the pattern.

Days of Creation Lace-Up Cards

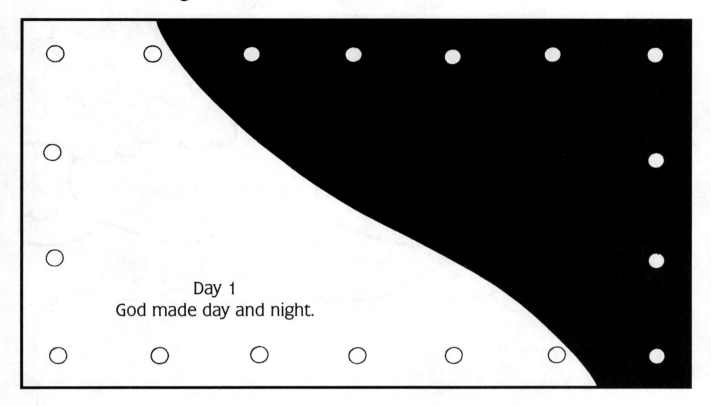

Day 1
God made day and night.

Day 2
God made the sky.

Days of Creation Lace-Up Card Patterns

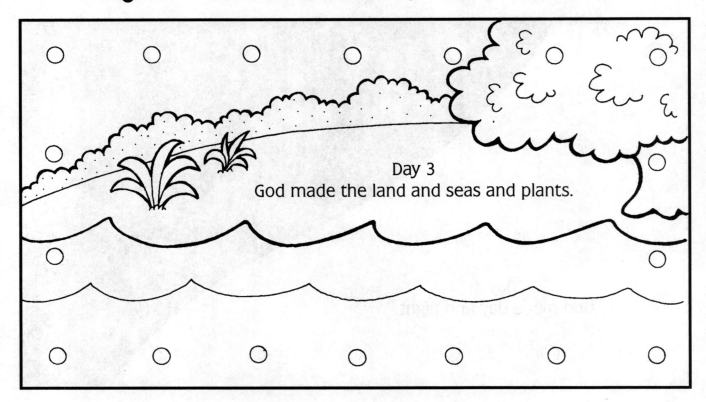

Day 3
God made the land and seas and plants.

Day 4
God made the sun, moon, and stars.

Days of Creation Lace-Up Card Patterns

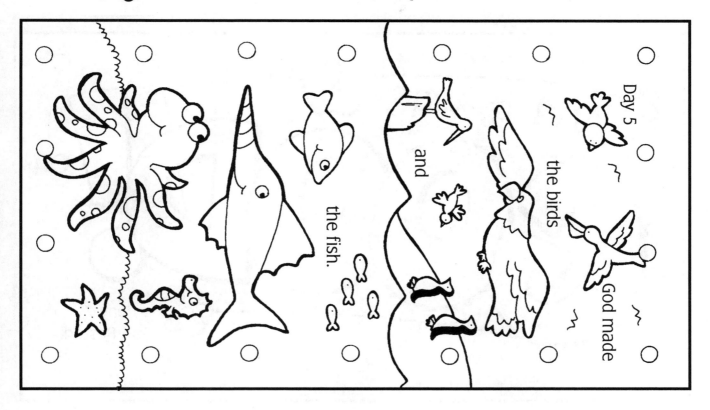

Day 5

the fish.

and

the birds

God made

Day 6

God made all the animals and people.

Days of Creation Lace-Up Card Pattern

And it was GOOD!

Day 7
God Rested.

Animals Two by Two

Genesis 1

The story of Noah and his ark is a favorite at any age. Coloring and placing all the animals on the deck of the ark will delight children.

Materials Needed:

* ✱ 12″ x 18″ brown construction paper
* ✱ White copy paper
* ✱ Crayons or markers
* ✱ Gluesticks
* ✱ Scissors

Directions:

1. Copy the ark pattern found on page 10. Color and cut it out.
2. Cut along the three dotted lines on the top and sides of the door and fold it open.
3. Copy the Bible verse pattern found on page 11 and cut it out.
4. Glue the ark and Bible verse onto the brown construction paper using the illustration on the right as your guide.
5. Copy the animal patterns found on pages 11–13. Color and cut out.
6. Glue animals onto the ark keeping in mind that some of them are still walking toward the ark and therefore will be glued to the "ground."

Genesis 6:19

You are to bring into the ark
two of all living creatures,
male and female,
to keep them alive with you.

Ark pattern

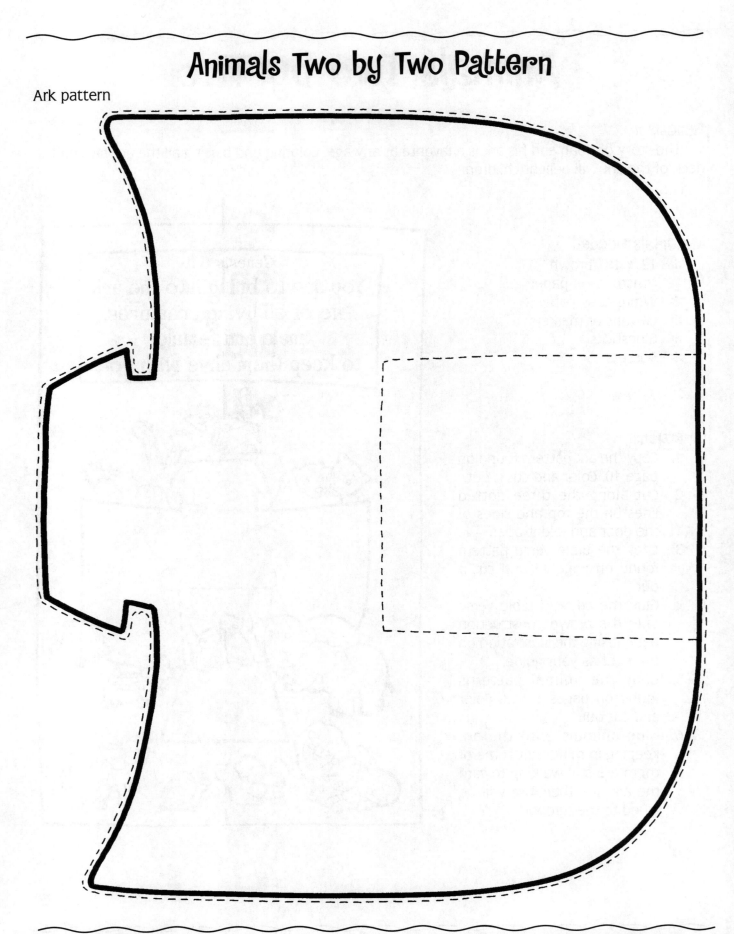

Genesis 6:19

You are to bring into the ark two of all living creatures, male and female, to keep them alive with you.

Animals Two by Two Patterns

Animals Two by Two Patterns

13

The Rainbow Promise

Genesis 6

A rainbow is a reminder from God that he will never again flood the earth. Using cotton balls as "paintbrushes," and dry tempera paint the children will be able to create their own rainbows.

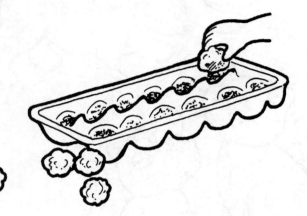

Materials Needed:

* White construction paper
  in two sizes 8.5˝x11˝ and 11˝x 18˝
* Large cotton balls
* Seven colors of tempera paint
  (pink, purple, red, orange,
  yellow, blue and green)
* Small trays or egg cartons for the paint
* Newspaper to cover work space

Directions:

1. Copy the rainbow pattern found on page 15 onto white construction paper. Cut it out.
2. Copy the ark pattern found on page 16. Color and cut out.
3. Glue the rainbow pattern in position on an 11˝ x 18˝ construction paper. Use the illustration above as your guide.
4. Cover the workspace with newspaper. Put a small amount of paint on the tray or in an egg carton.
5. Using a different cotton ball for every color, gently dab the cotton ball into the paint and color the rainbow.
6. After the rainbow is painted glue the ark under the rainbow. Use the illustration as your guide.
7. White cotton balls may be glued on the cloud patterns to give the project a 3-dimensional look.

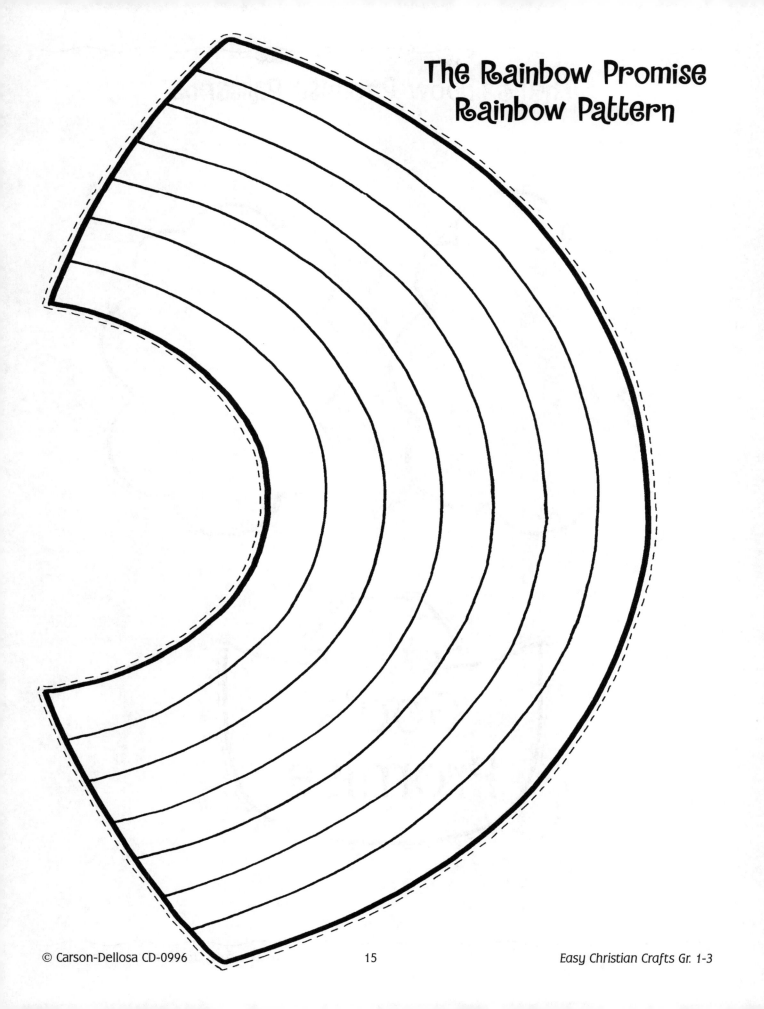

The Rainbow Promise
Rainbow Pattern

God's
Promise

Hiding God's Word in Your Heart

Deuteronomy 11:18

The Bible tells us to hide God's Word in our hearts. That means that when we read our Bibles we remember what it said and keep it close to us all the time so we won't forget. Children will love opening the heart on the paper person to find God's Word hidden there: the Bible!

Materials Needed:

* White construction paper
* Crayons
* Scissors
* Gluesticks
* Red paper
* *Optional:* Bible sticker

Directions:

1. Copy the Hiding God's Word in Your Heart pattern found on page 18.
2. Encourage the children to color the pattern to look like themselves.
3. Have the children color the Bible on the patterns, or you may use a Bible sticker to place over it. Make sure your sticker is not larger than the heart that will be placed over it.
4. Copy the heart pattern below onto red paper. Cut it out. Fold on the dotted line (the tab is the part that will be glued to the left of the Bible so the heart covers it.
5. Glue the heart flap on the person where indicated, making sure that you do not glue the actual heart, only the rectangle flap in place.

Heart pattern

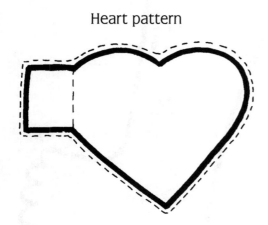

5. Glue the heart flap on the person.

Hiding God's Word in Your Heart

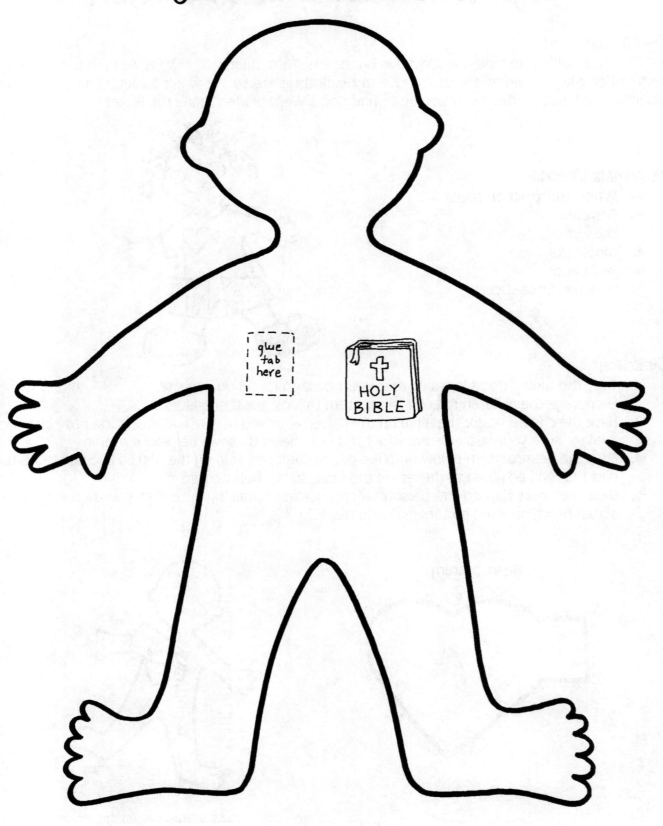

Moses' Basket

Exodus 2

Moses was a very special baby. God protected Moses by guiding his mother to place him in a basket among the reeds. God watches over each of us. Create a safe basket for baby Moses by gluing yarn to the reproducible picture on the following page.

Materials Needed:

* Yellow, gold, or brown yarn
* Glue or gluestick
* Heavy construction paper
* Crayons or markers
* Scissors

Directions:

1. Copy the pattern found on page 20. Cut it out.
2. Color the picture, but be careful not to color the basket. The wax from the crayon may prevent the glue from holding the yarn in place.
3. Glue the yarn onto the basket pattern.

Moses' Basket

Crossing on Dry Land

Exodus 13

In this favorite Bible story from the Old Testament, God leads and keeps Moses and his people safe while crossing the Red Sea. A simple shoe box theatre serves as the dry land for craft stick people to cross the Red Sea.

Materials Needed:

* 6 craft sticks
* Shoe box
* Crayons or markers
* Glue or gluestick
* scissors
* Brown and blue paint
* Newspaper
* *Optional:* Glitter

Directions:

1. Cover the work space with newspaper. Lay the shoe box on its side with the long side up. See step 1 below. Paint three sides of the box blue (water) and the top side brown (for dry land). Let the box dry completely.
2. Have an adult cut a slit in the middle across the top side of the shoe box (dry land).
3. Copy and color the patterns found on pages 22 and 23. Cut out.
4. Glue fish around the sides of the box to create the water being parted. *Note:* glitter may be used to decorate the fish.
5. Glue pattern pieces to the tops of the craft sticks, or tape the patterns on and use them as puppets.
6. Guide the sticks through the slit in the top of the shoe box so little hands can slide the people back and forth to "cross the Red Sea." When not in use, the box can be laid flat, with puppets inside, for storage.

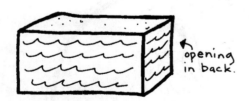

1. With the box on its side, paint three sides blue (water) and the top brown (for dry land).

5. Glue or tape pattern pieces to the tops of the craft sticks.

6. Guide the sticks through the slit in the top of the shoe box, so the children can slide the people back and forth.

Crossing on Dry Land

Friendship Frame

1 Samuel 20

David and Jonathan were the best of friends. This craft project will help children appreciate the importance of friends. Have the children put a picture of a friend in their own picture frame, or give the frame to a friend with a picture of themselves in it.

Materials Needed:

* ✳ Card stock, white or colored
* ✳ Scissors
* ✳ Crayons or markers
* ✳ Glue or gluestick

Directions:

1. Copy onto card stock the base frame pattern found on page 25.
2. Cut on the solid lines and fold in half on the dotted lines.
3. Copy onto card stock the top frame and stand patterns from page 26. Cut on the solid lines.
4. Color with markers or crayons.
5. Glue the bottom and sides of the top frame pattern to the base frame using step 5 below as your guide.
6. Fold stand on dotted lines and glue into place on the back of the base frame using step 6 below as your guide.
7. Slide your photograph through the opening in the top of the frame.

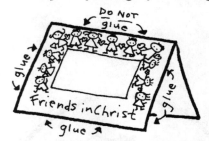

5. Glue the bottom and sides of the top frame pattern to the base frame.

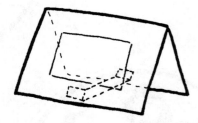

6. Fold stand on dotted lines and glue into place.

7. Slide your photograph through the opening in the top of the frame.

Friendship Base Frame Pattern

Friendship Frame Patterns

Top frame pattern

cut out

Friends in Christ

Stand pattern

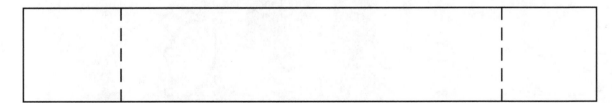

Daniel Stays Safe

Daniel 6

God kept Daniel safe in the lions' den because he did not listen to the king who told him to stop praying to God. Daniel never stopped praying or loving God. A moveable Daniel and lion will be fun for little hands to make and move.

Materials Needed:

* Brass fasteners
* Gold construction paper
* Crayons or markers
* Scissors
* White construction paper
* Paper punch

Directions:

1. Copy the lion pattern found on page 28 onto gold construction paper.
2. Copy the Daniel pattern found on page 29 onto white construction paper. Color the pattern.
3. Cut out the lion pattern and push fastener through the body parts as indicated on the pattern pieces. Do the same for the Daniel patterns.

Daniel Stays Safe Patterns

Lion patterns

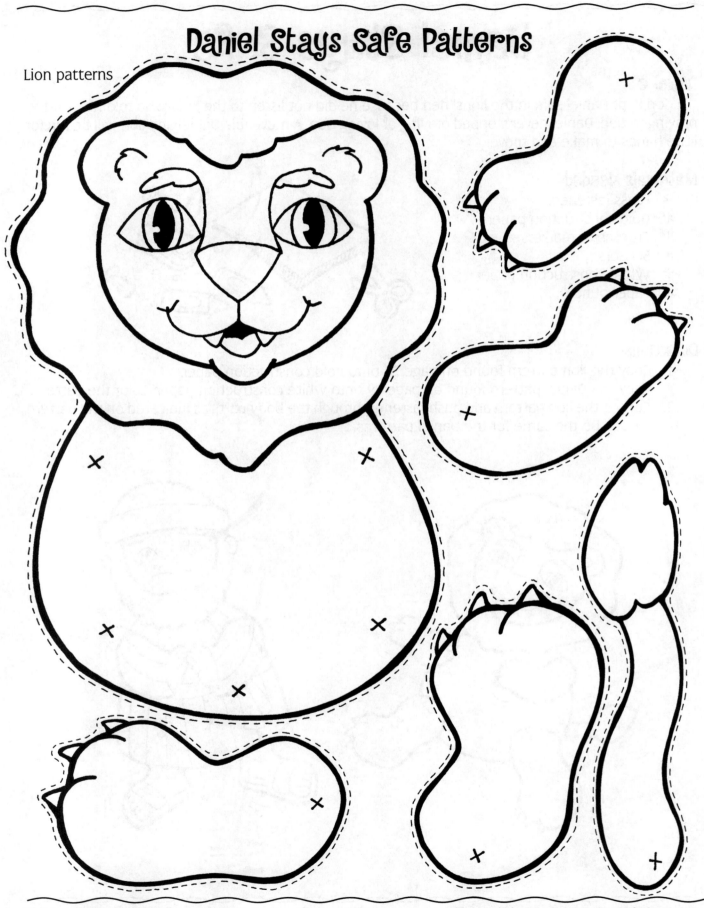

Daniel Stays Safe Patterns

Daniel patterns

Paper Bag Fish

Jonah

The story of Jonah and the big fish always delights young children. This story helps children realize that God always takes care of us. This project will make the children laugh. The paper bag fish "eats" Jonah and then spits him back out.

Materials Needed:

* White, lunch-size paper bag
* Stapler
* Crayons
* Self-stick Velcro Strip
* Newspaper
* Card stock
* *Optional:* wiggly eyes and glue

Directions:

1. Color the white bag to look like a fish. Use the illustration below as your guide. Expect the bag to become wrinkled as you color it, especially when drawing in the eyes and smile.
2. Stuff the fish with crumpled newspaper. Fold the opening over and staple closed.
3. Copy the Jonah pattern from the bottom of this page onto card stock, color, and cut out.
4. Cut a small piece of Velcro that will fit on the back of Jonah. Attach the other half of the velcro piece to the "mouth" of the big fish.
5. Attach Jonah to the fish when he is being "eaten" and remove him when he is being "spit-out."

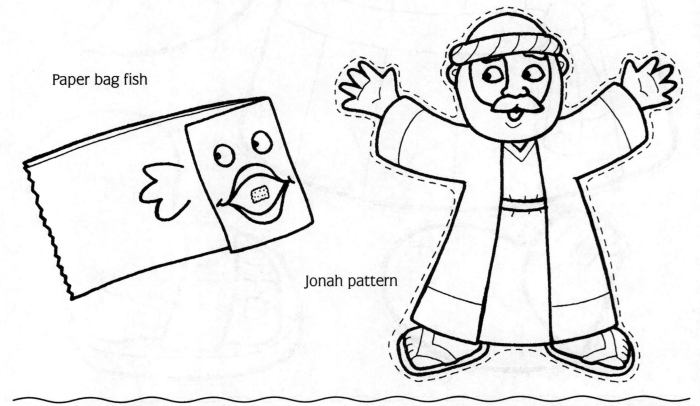

Paper bag fish

Jonah pattern

Paper Bag Nativity

Matthew 2

God's greatest act of love was sending his own son down to earth as a little baby who died and rose again to take away our sins. Little children will love to make their own grocery bag nativity set. They will spend hours telling and retelling the story of the birth of Jesus Christ.

Materials Needed:

* ✳ 2 brown grocery bags
* ✳ Heavy construction paper or card stock
* ✳ Self-stick Velcro Strip
* ✳ Scissors
* ✳ Crayons or markers
* ✳ *Optional:* yarn used for hay

Directions:

1. Open the two paper bags. Insert one open end into the other end. You should have a brown block with no sides open.
2. Cut an opening in one side of the "stable." (See illustration below.) Once you have cut through both bags you will need to tape the open end that is on the inside of the folded end.
3. Copy and cut from card stock or heavy construction paper the patterns found on pages 32–37.
4. Color the characters and fold patterns on the dotted lines toward the back of the pattern.
5. Arrange the characters in and outside of the stable. The stable can also be used for storage of the entire set.

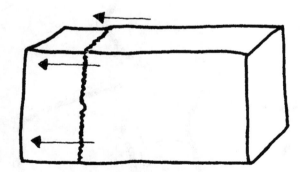

1. Insert one open end into the other end.

2. Cut an opening in one side of the "stable."

Paper Bag Nativity Patterns

Joseph pattern

Paper Bag Nativity Patterns

Mary pattern

Paper Bag Nativity Patterns

Sheep patterns

Paper Bag Nativity Patterns

Baby Jesus pattern

Paper Bag Nativity Patterns

Star pattern

Paper Bag Nativity Patterns

Shepherd pattern

Jesus Feeds 5000

Matthew 14:13-21

As believers, there is not a need of ours that God will not take care of. Stuffed paper made into five loaves of bread and two fish will help us remember that.

Materials Needed:
* Grocery bag
* Orange or light blue paper for fish
* Glitterglue
* Scissors
* Tape
* 5 small brown paper lunch bags
* Newspaper
* Stapler
* Crayons or markers

Directions:
1. To make the basket, use a large grocery bag. Cut each side of the bag down 6˝ and fold. Tape around each corner to reinforce.
2. Using another grocery bag, cut out a 24˝ handle and staple to the inside of the basket.
3. Copy two of each fish patterns found on pages 39 and 40 onto colored paper. Cut out the pattern.
4. Decorate the fish with glitterglue or markers as desired.
5. To prepare the fish for stuffing, close the edges of the fish by stapling two of the same patterns together approximately 3/4˝ around the edge.
6. Crumple newspaper and stuff the fish. Staple closed and place in the basket.
7. To make bread, open a lunch bag. Crumple newspaper into loaf shapes and stuff into the bag. Mold the bag around the newspaper to form a loaf of bread. Fold the opening over twice and staple closed. Make fives loaves and place in the basket with the fish.

1. Tape around each corner to reinforce. Add the handle.

7. Hands molding bag into bread loaf.

5. To prepare the fish for stuffing, close the edges of the fish by stapling two of the same patterns together approximately 3/4˝ around the edge.

Jesus Feeds 5000 Pattern

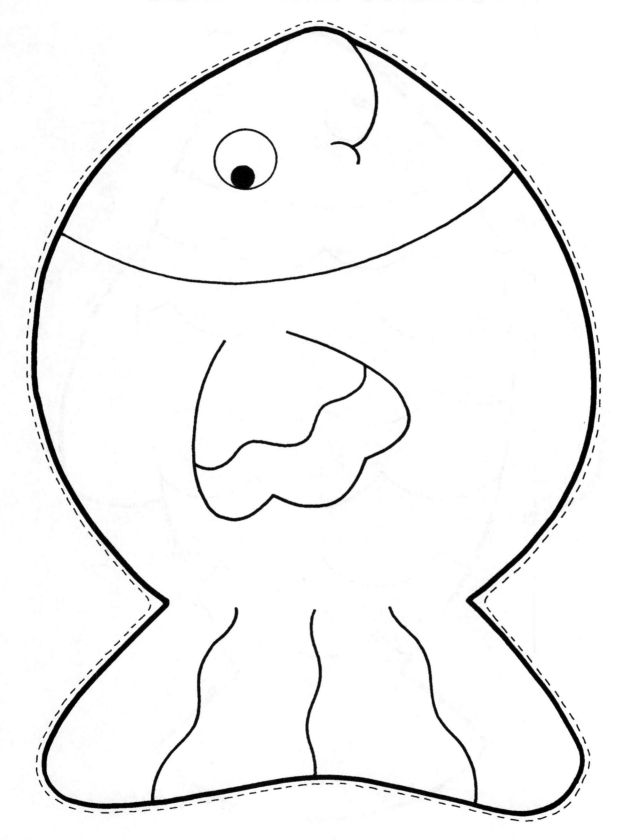

Jesus Feeds 5000 Pattern

Easy Christian Crafts Preschool/Kindergarten

Triumphal Entry Palm Branch

Matthew 21

Jesus was hailed as King as he rode into Jerusalem on a donkey. This simple palm branch will be waved with praise to our King!

Materials Needed:

* Green construction paper (if you want to color the branch use white paper)
* Tape or gluesticks
* Scissors

Directions:

1. Copy the palm branch patterns found on pages 41 and 42 onto green construction paper.
2. Cut pattern out on dotted lines.
3. Tape or glue together where indicated.
4. Wave the palm branch and praise Jesus!

Triumphal Entry Palm Branch Pattern
(top half)

Triumphal Entry Palm Branch Pattern

(bottom half)

Paper Plate Tomb

Mark 16

When Mary Magdalene and Mary the mother of James reached the tomb where Jesus was buried, they saw that the stone had been rolled away and that an angel sat inside the tomb. The children will be able to roll the stone away from their own paper plate tomb.

Materials Needed:
* ✳ Paper plate
* ✳ Card stock
* ✳ Scissors
* ✳ Gluestick
* ✳ Brass fasteners
* ✳ Crayons or markers

Directions:
1. Copy the inside tomb pattern found on page 44.
2. Copy the stone pattern found on page 45 onto card stock.
3. Color each pattern. Cut out on the dotted lines.
4. Glue the inside of the tomb pattern to the center of the paper plate.
5. Holding the stone pattern in one hand, push the brass fastener through it where it is indicated on the pattern.
6. Push the fastener (already through the stone) through the paper plate where indicated on the pattern.
7. Roll the stone away from the tomb opening and see that Jesus is indeed alive!

4. Glue the inside of the tomb pattern to the center of the paper plate.

5. Holding the stone pattern in one hand, push the brass fastener through it where it is indicated on the pattern.

6. Push the fastener (already through the stone) through the paper plate where indicated on the pattern.

7. Roll the stone away from the tomb opening and see that Jesus is indeed alive!

Paper Plate Tomb Pattern

Inside Tomb pattern

Paper Plate Tomb Pattern

Stone pattern – copy onto card stock

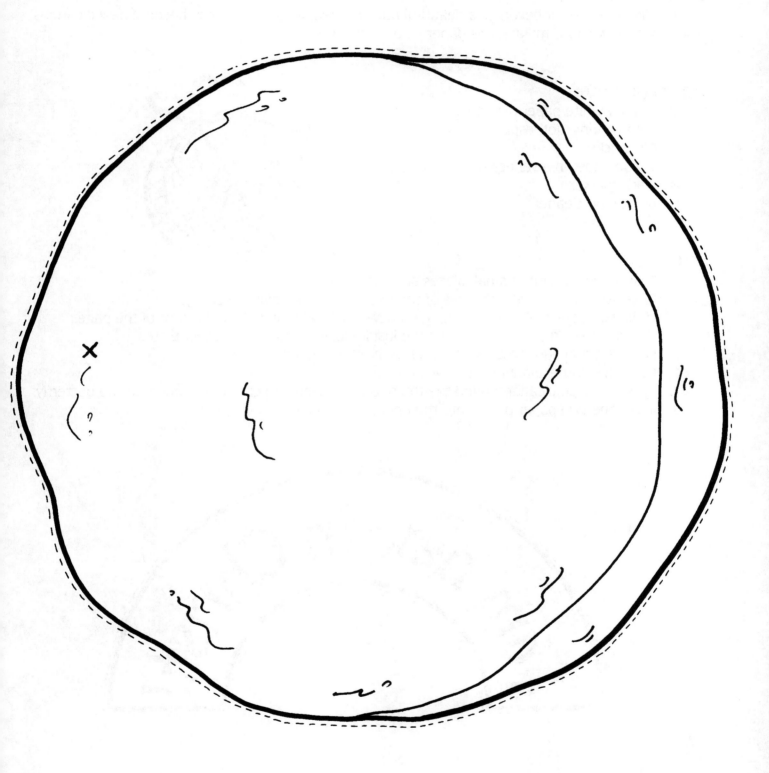

I Am New in Christ Butterfly

2 Corinthians 5:17

Just like a caterpillar becomes a beautiful butterfly, we, who are in Christ, become new creations also! Children will love making this paper plate butterfly.

Materials Needed:
* 2 small white paper plates
* 1 non-spring clothespin
* Gluesticks
* Tissue paper in a variety of colors
* Black marker
* Black pipe cleaner

Directions:
1. Tear tissue paper into small pieces and set aside.
2. Glue tissue paper on both sides of the two small paper plates. Let dry.
3. Make two copies of the pattern, "I am new in Christ" found at the bottom of the page.
4. Glue the patterns in a circle along the inside ridge of one of the paper plates.
5. Place the two paper plates on top of each other and fold in half.
6. Color the clothespin with the black marker.
7. Twist the pipe cleaner around the top of the clothespin to create antennae for the butterfly.
8. Insert the two paper plates into the opening of the clothespin.

I Am New in Christ pattern

Fruit of the Spirit Basket

Galatians 5:22

We are to live by the spirit. This paper fruit basket can help explain to young children what is meant by living with the fruit of the spirit.

Materials Needed:

* Brown construction paper
* 12˝ x 18˝ white construction paper
* White or colored construction paper (red, green, yellow, orange)
* Scissors
* Crayons or markers
* Gluesticks

Directions:

1. Copy the basket pattern from page 48 onto brown construction paper. Cut it out.
2. Copy the fruit patterns from pages 49 and 50 onto white construction paper. The patterns may also be copied onto colored construction paper.
3. If you copied the fruit patterns on white paper, color them and cut them out.
4. Using the diagram below as your guide, glue the basket onto the 12˝ x 18˝ piece of construction paper.
5. Glue the fruit inside and laying next to the basket.

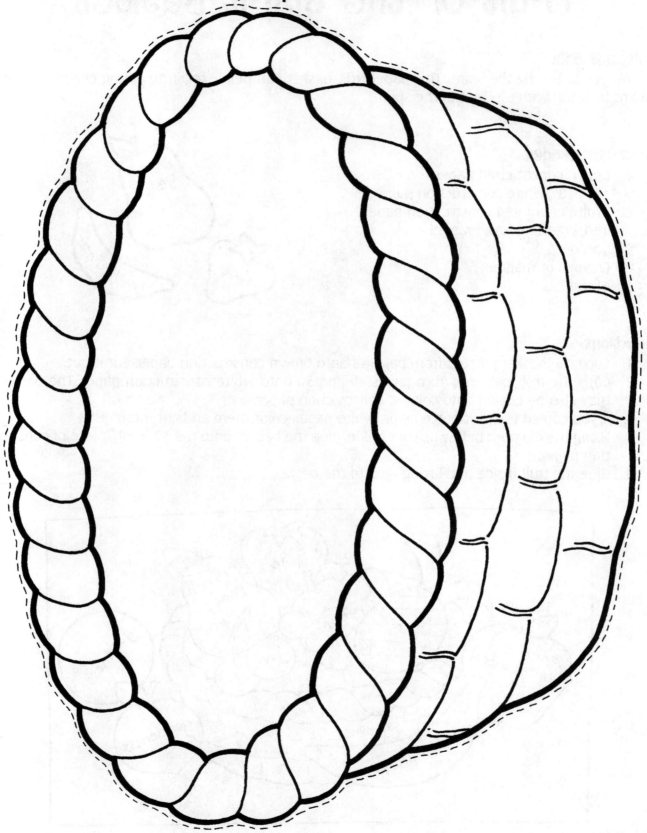

Fruit of the Spirit Fruit Patterns

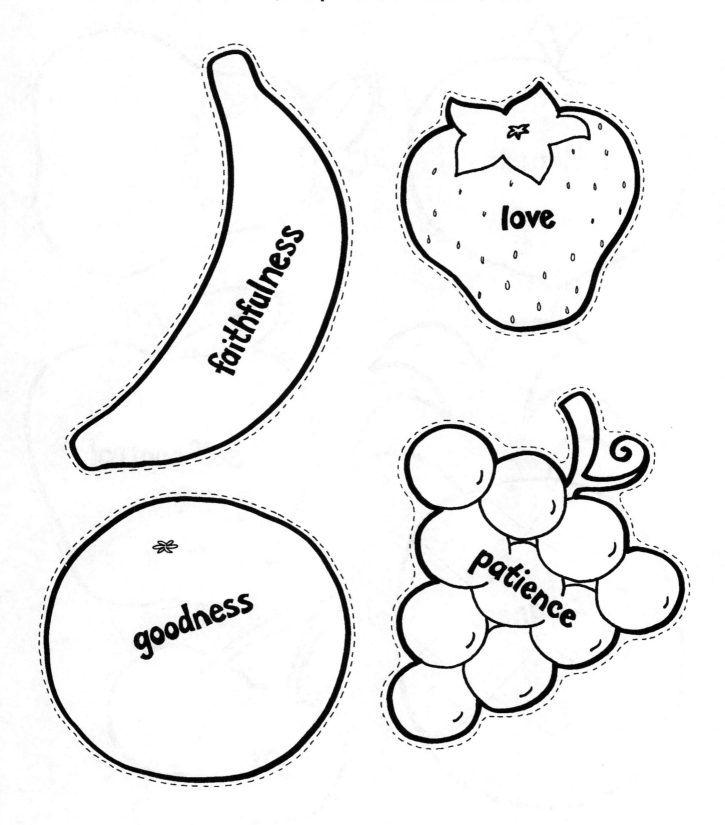

Fruit of the Spirit Fruit Patterns

gentleness

peace

self-control

kindness

joy

Paul's Chain of Love

Philippians 1:12

Even though Paul was in prison, his love for God stayed strong and God used Paul to spread His Good News. Creating paper chains is an easy project and a great way for us to remember that wherever we are, we can tell others about Jesus' love.

Materials Needed:

* Colored construction paper
* Scissors
* Gluesticks

Directions:

1. Copy the chain patterns found on pages 52–54. Cut along the dotted lines.
2. Roll the first strip to make a loop for your chain and glue the ends together, making sure that the writing is showing on the outside of the chain.
3. Thread the next strip through the first loop and glue the ends together, again making sure that the writing is on the outside of the chain.
4. Continue step three until you have the desired length of chain.
5. From the chain, read the truths and promises that Paul remembered while he was in prison, and encourage the children to repeat some of them.

Paul's Chain of Love Patterns

God is always loving me!

Jesus loves me!

I will always pray!

I love Jesus!

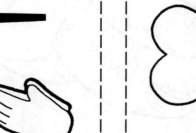

Jesus is my best friend!

I pray for my friends.

Jesus is in my heart!

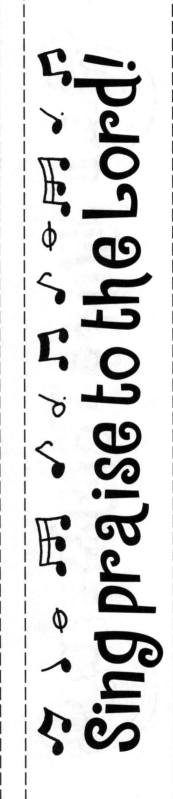

Sing praise to the Lord!

Paul's Chain of Love Patterns

God loves me!

I worship God.

God is love.

Tell others about Jesus

 Easy Christian Crafts Preschool/Kindergarten

I Am Jesus' Light

Ephesians 5:8

For you were once in darkness, but now you are light in the Lord. Live as children of light. Children will love to let their light shine with these paper towel tube candles.

Materials Needed:
* ❋ Paper towel tube
* ❋ Glue stick
* ❋ Red, orange, and yellow tissue paper
* ❋ Colored construction paper

Directions:
1. Copy the candle base pattern found on page 56 onto colored construction paper. Cut out the pattern along the solid lines.
2. Wrap the construction paper pattern around a paper towel tube and glue in place.
3. Cut red, orange, and yellow tissue paper into 6˝ x 6˝ squares. Stuff the tissue paper squares into the end of the tube to create a pretend flame.

I Am Jesus' Light Candle Base Pattern

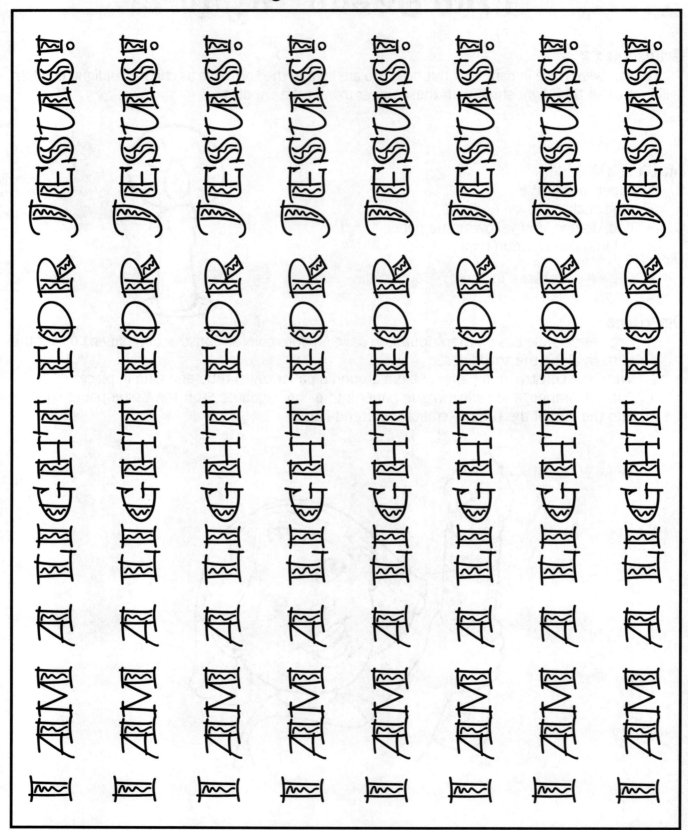

Dressed in Armor

Ephesians 6:13–17

Paul tells us that we need to stay strong in our faith. We can do this by learning about and wearing the "Armor of God." This project will help young children begin to understand how the Armor of God can protect us.

Materials Needed:

* ✳ Card stock or white copy paper
* ✳ Crayons or markers
* ✳ Glue or glue sticks
* ✳ Scissors

Directions:

1. Copy the "Dressed in Armor" boy pattern found on page 58 or the "Dressed in Armor" girl pattern found on page 59 onto card stock or white paper.
2. These pages can be used as a coloring activity.
3. Copy the armor patterns found on page 60 onto white paper. These patterns can be used to turn this project into a cut and glue activity.
4. Cut out the patterns and glue them on top of the matching piece of armor on the boy or girl pattern.
5. The picture may be colored after the glue has dried.

Dressed in Armor Boy Pattern

sword of the **SPIRIT**

helmet of
SALVATION

breastplate of
RIGHTEOUSNESS

shield of
FAITH

belt of
TRUTH

gospel of
PEACE

gospel of
PEACE

Dressed in Armor Girl Pattern

sword of the **SPIRIT**

helmet of
SALVATION

breastplate of
RIGHTEOUSNESS

shield of
FAITH

belt of
TRUTH

gospel of
PEACE

gospel of
PEACE

Dressed in Armor Patterns

shield of
FAITH

sword of the
SPIRIT

belt of
TRUTH

breastplate of
RIGHTEOUSNESS

glue belt here

cut out

helmet of
SALVATION

gospel of
PEACE

gospel of
PEACE

Crown of Life

Revelation 2:10

Jesus tells us that if we are faithful he will give us the crown of life. Children will love making and wearing their own "crown of life."

Materials Needed:

* ✻ 2 sheets of card stock
* ✻ *Crown decorations:* Self-adhesive jewels, colored construction paper, crayons and markers, and glitter
* ✻ Stapler
* ✻ Tape
* ✻ Scissors

Directions:

1. Copy the crown and jewel patterns found on pages 62 and 63 onto card stock.
2. Cut out the patterns along the dotted lines
3.. Tape or glue the two crown patterns together as indicted.
4. Decorate the crown using the above listed materials.
5. Wrap the decorated crown around the child's head and tape or staple the two ends together.

Crown of Life Patterns

tape   tape   tape

Crown of Life Patterns

God's Love Shines

2 Corinthians 4:6

God wants us to let his light shine! Children will delight in watching their crayon "light" shine through as they apply dark paint.

Materials Needed:
* White construction paper
* Black, purple, or dark blue watercolor
* Crayons
* Newspaper
* Paint shirts to cover clothing

Directions:
1. Cover the work area with newspaper and provide the children paint shirts to wear.
2. Have the children draw and color a picture of a candle. Encourage the children to press firmly as they color.
3. When the picture has been colored, paint over the entire picture with a dark watercolor. The wax of the crayon will repel the paint causing the candle to "shine through."
4. Let the picture dry completely.